PIANO • VOCAL • GUITAR

THE GRAMMY

SONG OF THE YEAR

1990 – 1999

GRAMMY, GRAMMY Awards and the gramophone logo are registered
trademarks of The Recording Academy® and are used under license.

Visit The Recording Academy Online at
www.grammy.com

ISBN 978-1-4584-1560-8

HAL•LEONARD®
CORPORATION

7777 W. BLUEMOUND RD. P.O. BOX 13819 MILWAUKEE, WI 53213

Visit Hal Leonard Online at
www.halleonard.com

» Adele at the 54th GRAMMY Awards

THE RECORDING ACADEMY®

When it comes to music on TV, the last few years alone have seen some very memorable moments: Paul McCartney, Bruce Springsteen, Dave Grohl, and Joe Walsh jamming on "The End" from the Beatles' classic *Abbey Road*; Adele making her triumphant first live singing appearance after throat surgery to perform "Rolling In The Deep"; Pink dripping wet and hovering 20 feet above the stage while singing a note-perfect version of "Glitter In The Air"; and Lady Gaga hatching from a massive egg to perform "Born This Way." All of these performances, and many more, took place on the famed GRAMMY Awards® stage.

The GRAMMY® Award is indisputedly the most sought-after recognition of excellence in recorded music worldwide. Over more than half a century, the GRAMMY Awards have become both music's biggest honor and Music's Biggest Night®, with the annual telecast drawing tens of millions of viewers nationwide and millions more internationally.

And with evolving categories that always reflect important current artistic waves — such as dance/electronica music — as well as setting a record for social TV engagement in 2012, the GRAMMYs keep moving forward, serving as a real-time barometer of music's cultural impact.

The Recording Academy is the organization that produces the GRAMMY Awards. Consisting of the artists, musicians, songwriters, producers, engineers, and other professionals who make the music you enjoy every day on the radio, your streaming or download services, or in the concert hall, The Academy is a dynamic institution with an active agenda aimed at supporting and nurturing music and the people who make it.

Whether it's joining with recording artists to ensure their creative rights are protected, providing ongoing professional development services to the recording community or supporting the health and well-being of music creators and music education in our schools, The Recording Academy has become the recording industry's primary organization for professional and educational outreach, human services, arts advocacy, and cultural enrichment.

The Academy represents members from all corners of the professional music world — from the biggest recording stars to unsung music educators — all brought together under the banner of building a better creative environment for music and its makers.

» Paul McCartney at the 2012 MusiCares Person of the Year gala in his honor — Christopher Polk/WireImage.com

» Trombone Shorty and Mavis Staples at the GRAMMY Foundation's Music Preservation Project event in 2012 — Michael Kovac/WireImage.com

MUSICARES FOUNDATION®

MusiCares® was established by The Recording Academy to provide a safety net of critical assistance for music people in times of need. MusiCares has developed into a premier support system for music people, providing resources to cover a wide range of financial, medical and personal emergencies through innovative programs and services, including regular eBay auctions of one-of-a-kind memorabilia that are open to the public. The charity has been supported by the contributions and participation of artists such as Neil Diamond, Aretha Franklin, Paul McCartney, Bruce Springsteen, Barbra Streisand, and Neil Young — just to name the organization's most recent annual Person of the Year fundraiser honorees — and so many others through the years.

THE GRAMMY FOUNDATION®

The GRAMMY Foundation's mission is to cultivate the understanding, appreciation and advancement of the contribution of recorded music to American culture. The Foundation accomplishes this mission through programs and activities designed to engage the music industry and cultural community as well as the general public. The Foundation works to bring national attention to important issues such as the value and impact of music and arts education and the urgency of preserving our rich cultural legacy, and it accomplishes this work by engaging music professionals — from big-name stars to working professionals and educators — to work directly with students.

≫ Secretary of the Department of Health and Human Services Kathleen Sebelius and Recording Academy President/CEO Neil Portnow present the Recording Artists' Coalition Award to John Mayer at the GRAMMYs on the Hill Awards in Washington, D.C., in 2012

Paul Morigi/WireImage.com

FIGHTING FOR MUSICIANS' RIGHTS

Over the last 15 years, The Recording Academy has built a presence in the nation's capital, working to amplify the voice of music creators in national policy matters. Today, called the "supersized musicians lobby" by *Congressional Quarterly*, The Academy's Advocacy & Industry Relations office in Washington, D.C., is the leading representative of the collective world of recording professionals — artists, songwriters, producers, and engineers — through its GRAMMYs on the Hill® Initiative. The Academy has taken a leadership role in the fight to expand radio performance royalties to all music creators, worked on behalf of musicians on censorship concerns and regularly supported musicians on legislative issues that impact the vitality of music.

THE GRAMMY MUSEUM®

Since opening its doors in December 2008, the GRAMMY Museum has served as a dynamic educational and interactive institution dedicated to the power of music. The four-story, 30,000-square foot facility is part of L.A. Live, the premier sports and entertainment destination in downtown Los Angeles. The Museum serves the community with interactive, permanent and traveling exhibits and an array of public and education programs. We invite you to visit us when you're in the Los Angeles area.

As you can see, The Recording Academy is so much more than the annual GRAMMY telecast once a year, even if that one show is Music's Biggest Night. To keep up with all The Academy's activities, visit GRAMMY.com regularly, and join the conversation on our social networks:

 Facebook.com/TheGRAMMYs

 Twitter.com/TheGRAMMYs

 YouTube.com/TheGRAMMYs

 TheGRAMMYs.tumblr.com

 Foursquare.com/TheGRAMMYs

 Instagram (user name: TheGRAMMYs)

 Google+ (gplus.to/TheGRAMMYs)

TABLE OF CONTENTS (ALPHABETICAL)

TABLE OF CONTENTS (CHRONOLOGICAL)

🏆 WINNER

*Omitted due to licensing restrictions.

ACHY BREAKY HEART
(Don't Tell My Heart)

Words and Music by
DON VON TRESS

might blow _ up and kill this man. Ooh. _____

Don't tell my heart, my ach-y break-y heart. _ I just don't think he'd un-der-

stand. And if you tell my heart, my ach-y break-y heart, _ he

might blow _ up and kill this man. Ooh. _____

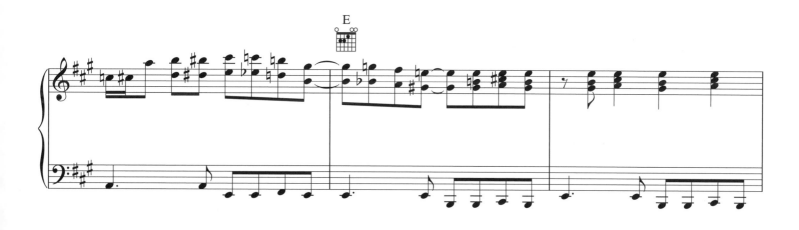

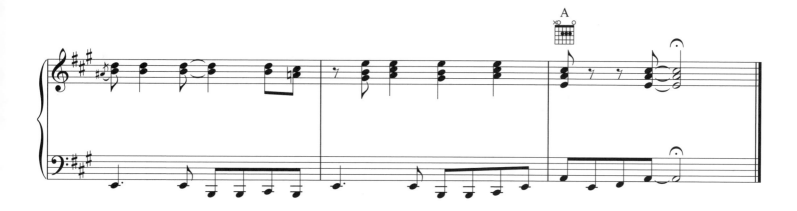

ALL I WANNA DO

Words and Music by KEVIN GILBERT,
DAVID BAERWALD, SHERYL CROW,
WYN COOPER and BILL BOTTRELL

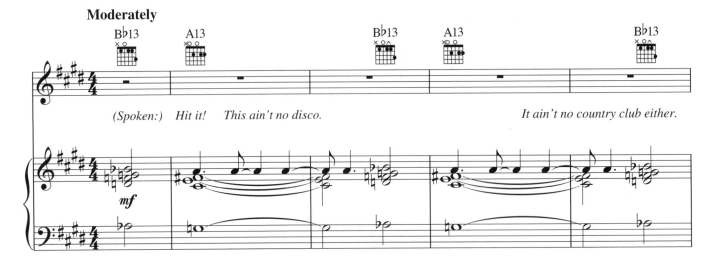

Additional Lyrics

3. I like a good beer buzz early in the morning,
  And Billy likes to peel the labels from his bottles of Bud
  And shred them on the bar.
  Then he lights every match in an oversized pack,
  Letting each one burn down to his thick fingers
  Before blowing and cursing them out.
  And he's watching the Buds as they spin on the floor.
  A happy couple enters the bar dancing dangerously close to one another.
  The bartender looks up from his want ads.
  Chorus

ANOTHER DAY IN PARADISE

Words and Music by
PHIL COLLINS

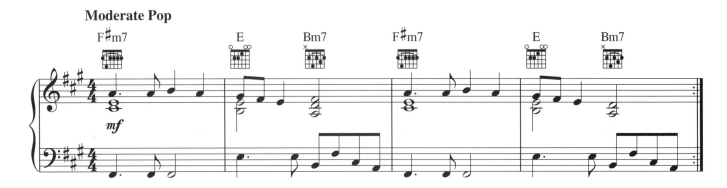

She calls out ___ to the man ___ on the street, ___ "Sir, ___ can you help ___
He walks on, ___ does - n't look back. ___ He pre - tends ___ he can't hear ___
She calls out ___ to the man ___ on the street. ___ He can see ___ she's been cry -
You can tell ___ from the lines ___ on her face. ___ You can see ___ that she's been

___ me? It's cold ___ and I've no - where to sleep.
___ her. Starts to whis - tle as he cross - es the street.
- ing. She's got blis - ters on the soles ___ of her feet. ___
___ there. Prob - a - bly been moved on from ev - er - y place ___

BABY BABY

Words and Music by AMY GRANT
and KEITH THOMAS

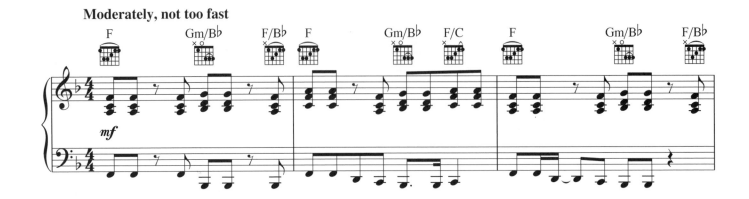

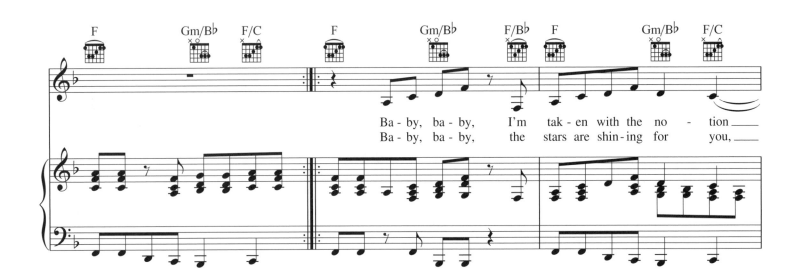

Baby, baby, I'm tak-en with the no - tion ____
Baby, baby, the stars are shin-ing for you, ____

____ to love you with the sweet-est of de - vo - tion. ____ Ba - by, ba - by, my
____ and just like me, I'm sure that they a - dore you. ____ Ba - by, ba - by, go

BEAUTY AND THE BEAST

from Walt Disney's BEAUTY AND THE BEAST

Lyrics by HOWARD ASHMAN
Music by ALAN MENKEN

BECAUSE YOU LOVED ME

Words and Music by
DIANE WARREN

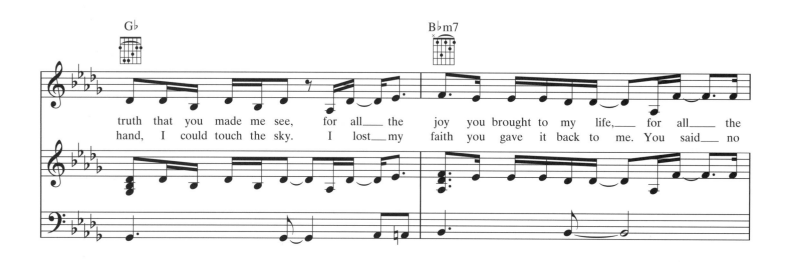

DON'T SPEAK

Words and Music by ERIC STEFANI
and GWEN STEFANI

Moderately

You and me, we used to be to-geth - er, ev-'ry day to-geth - er, al -

- ways. I real-ly feel ____ that I'm los - ing my best ___ friend. I

can't be-lieve this could ___ be the ___ end. It looks as though ___ you're ___
As we die, ___ both ___

BLUE

Words and Music by
BILL MACK

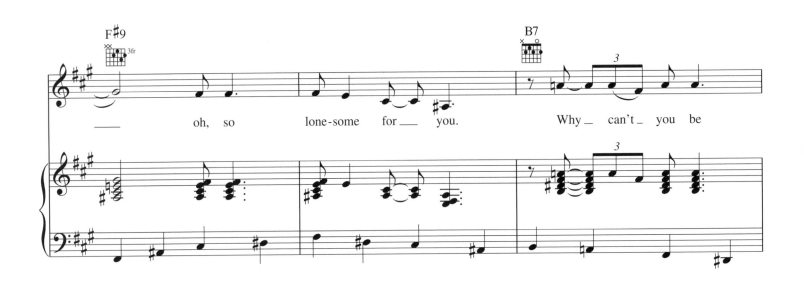

CAN YOU FEEL THE LOVE TONIGHT

from Walt Disney Pictures' THE LION KING

Music by ELTON JOHN
Lyrics by TIM RICE

CHANGE THE WORLD

featured on the Motion Picture Soundtrack PHENOMENON

Words and Music by WAYNE KIRKPATRICK,
GORDON KENNEDY and TOMMY SIMS

Moderately, not too fast

If I can reach the stars,
If I could be king,

pull one down for you,
e - ven for a day,

CIRCLE OF LIFE
from Walt Disney Pictures' THE LION KING

Music by ELTON JOHN
Lyrics by TIM RICE

Relaxed Pop beat

From the

CONSTANT CRAVING

Words and Music by k.d. lang
and BEN MINK

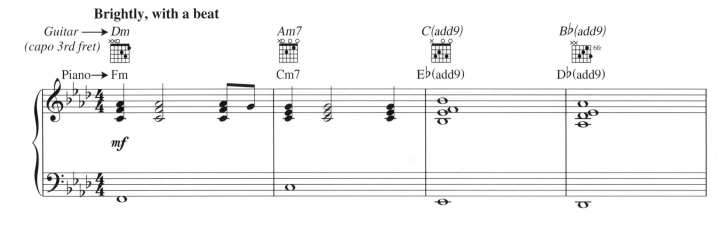

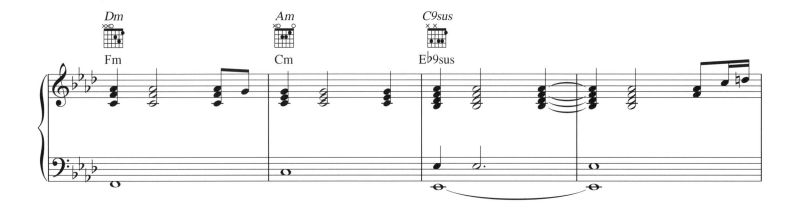

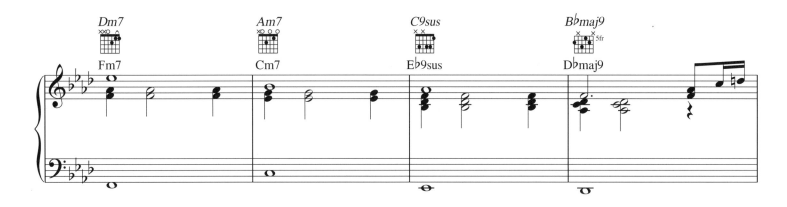

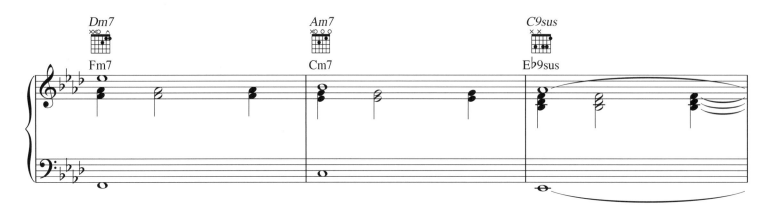

(Everything I Do)
I DO IT FOR YOU

from the Motion Picture ROBIN HOOD: PRINCE OF THIEVES

Words and Music by BRYAN ADAMS,
R.J. LANGE and MICHAEL KAMEN

EXHALE
(Shoop Shoop)
from the Original Soundtrack Album WAITING TO EXHALE

Words and Music by
BABYFACE

Easy R&B Ballad

(1.) Ev - 'ry - one falls in love some - times. _____ Some - times it's
(2.,3.) laugh, some - times you'll cry. _____ Life nev - er

wrong _____ and some - times it's right. For ev - 'ry
tells __ us __ the whens or whys. When you've got

win some - one must fail, but there comes a
friends to wish you well, you'll find a

FROM A DISTANCE

Words and Music by
JULIE GOLD

GIVE ME ONE REASON

Words and Music by
TRACY CHAPMAN

Medium Blues

Tune guitar down one half step.

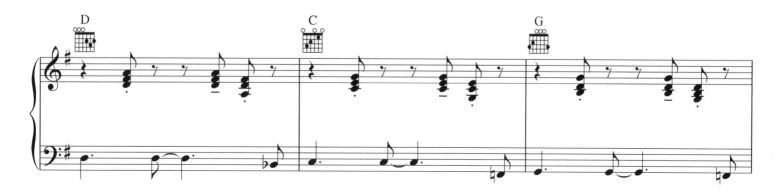

Give me one rea-son to stay here and I'll turn right back a - round.

Give me one rea-son to stay here and I'll turn right back a - round. Said I

don't want to leave you _ lone- ly; _ you _ got to make me change my _ mind. _

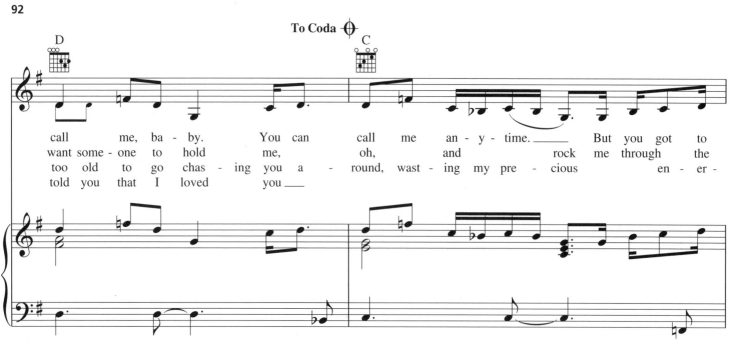

call me, baby. You can call me an-y-time._____ But you got to
want some-one to hold me, oh, and rock me through the
too old to go chas-ing you a-round, wast-ing my pre-cious en-er-

call_____ me.
night. _____
gy. _____

(You could see me turn-ing.)

HOLD ON

Words and Music by CARNIE WILSON,
CHYNNA PHILLIPS and GLEN BALLARD

HOW DO I LIVE

Words and Music by
DIANE WARREN

with-out you?

Verse 2:
Without you, there'd be no sun in my sky,
There would be no love in my life,
There'd be no world left for me.
And I, baby, I don't know what I would do,
I'd be lost if I lost you.
If you ever leave,
Baby, you would take away everything real in my life.
And tell me now,
(To Chorus:)

I CAN LOVE YOU LIKE THAT

Words and Music by MARIBETH DERRY,
JENNIFER KIMBALL and STEVE DIAMOND

I BELIEVE I CAN FLY

from SPACE JAM

Words and Music by
ROBERT KELLY

I DON'T WANT TO MISS A THING

Words and Music by
DIANE WARREN

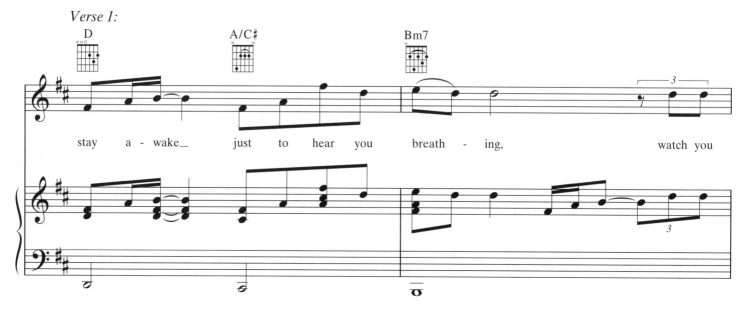

I SWEAR

Words and Music by FRANK MYERS
and GARY BAKER

I see the ques - tions in ____ your eyes; ____ I know what's weigh -
I'll give you ev - 'ry - thing ___ I can; ____ I'll build your dreams ___

I WANT IT THAT WAY

Words and Music by MAX MARTIN
and ANDREAS CARLSSON

I'D DO ANYTHING FOR LOVE
(But I Won't Do That)

Words and Music by
JIM STEINMAN

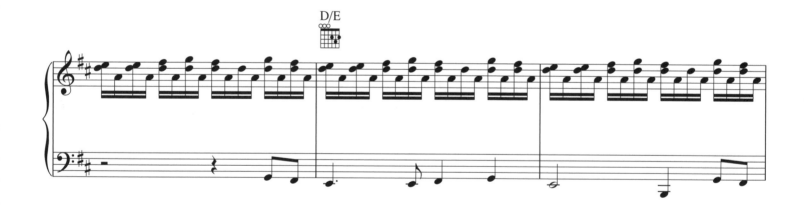

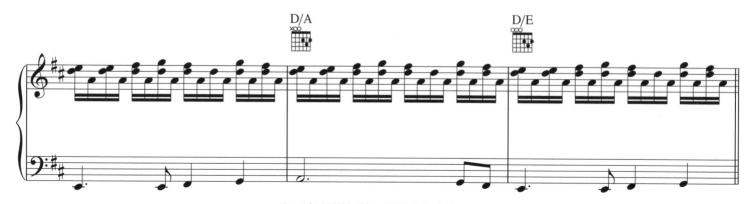

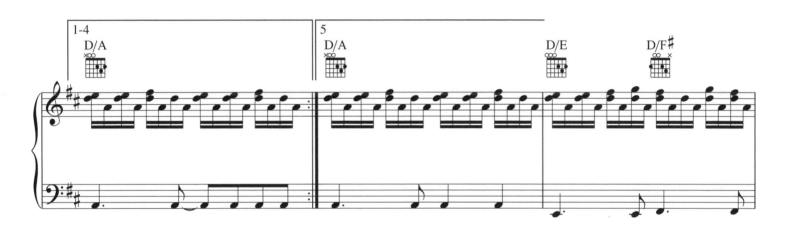

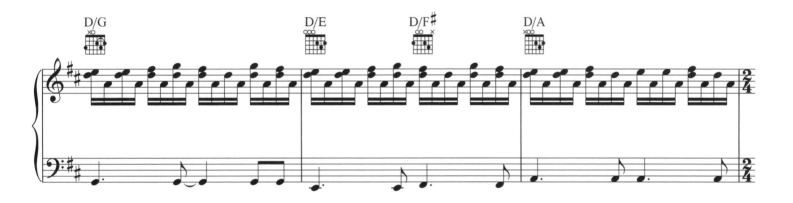

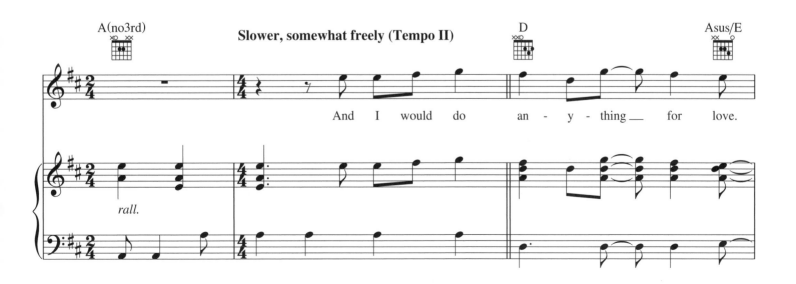

LEAN ON ME

Words and Music by
KIRK FRANKLIN

Moderately, with emotion

Spoken: This is for that little child with no father, for that man that doesn't have a place to stay, and for that little boy living with AIDS— you can lean on me.

154

IF I EVER LOSE MY FAITH IN YOU

Music and Lyrics by
STING

You could say I lost__ my faith in__ sci-
Some would say I was__ a lost__ man in a__ lost
I nev-er saw no mir-a-cle of sci-ence

-ence and prog-ress.
world.

IRIS
from the Motion Picture CITY OF ANGELS

Words and Music by
JOHN RZEZNIK

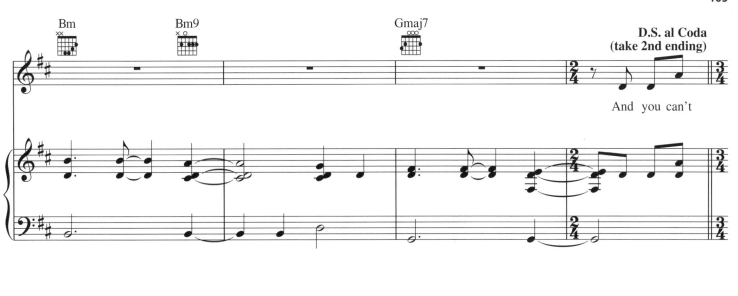

D.S. al Coda
(take 2nd ending)

And you can't

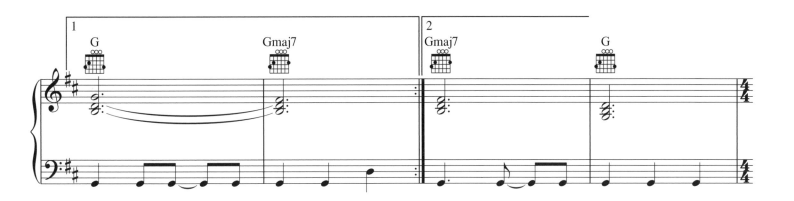

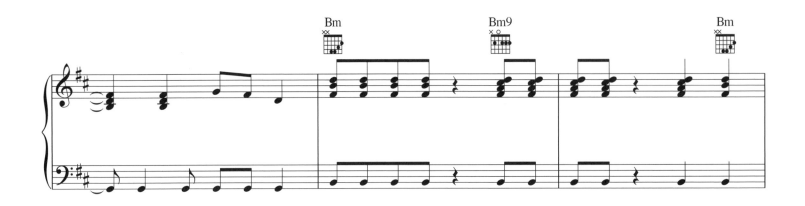

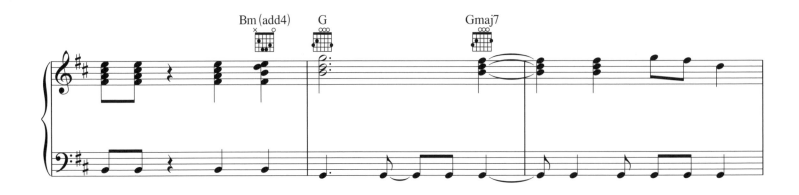

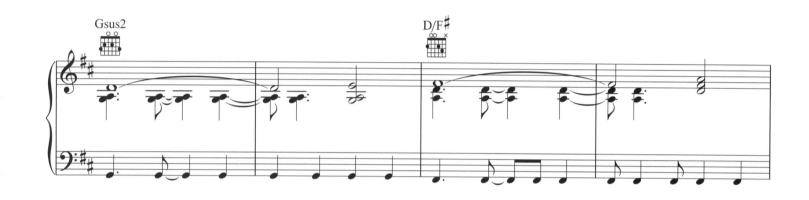

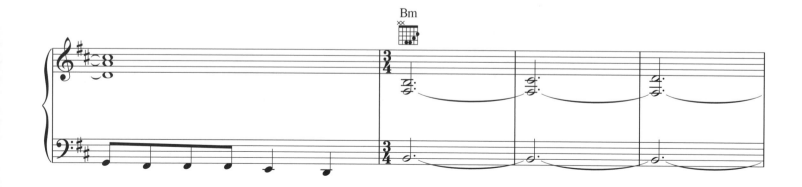

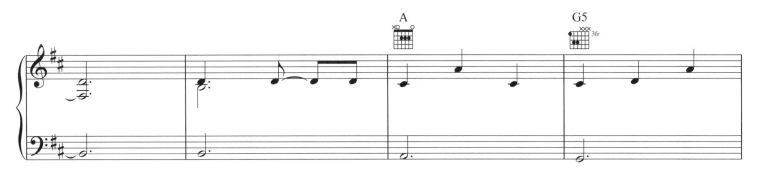

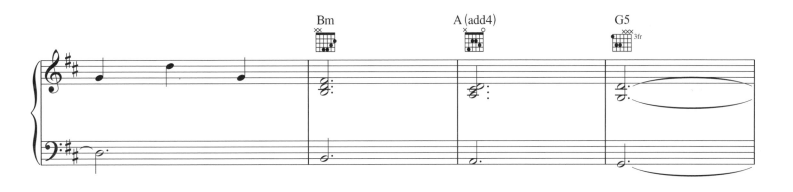

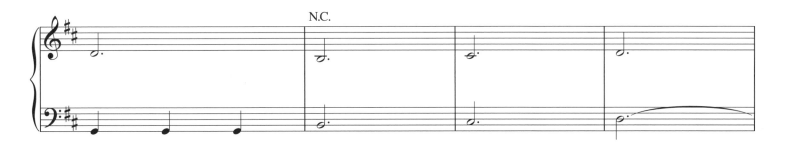

And I _____ don't want the world _____ to see _____ me

KISS FROM A ROSE

Words and Music by
SEAL

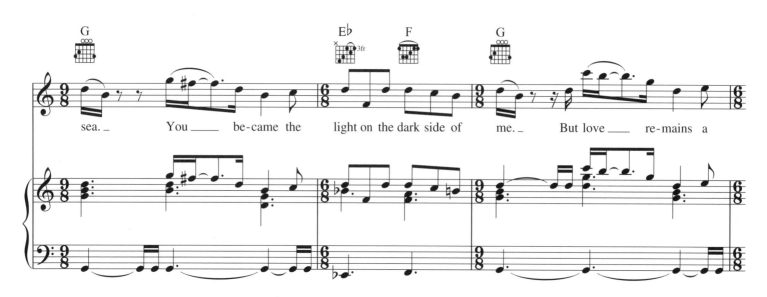

LIVIN' LA VIDA LOCA

Words and Music by DESMOND CHILD
and ROBI ROSA

She's in-to su-per-sti-tions, black cats and

voo-doo dolls. __ I feel a prem-o-ni-tion.

That girl's gon-na make me fall. __

She's liv-in' la vi - da lo - ca.

Play 3 times

Liv-in' la vi - da lo - ca. A-

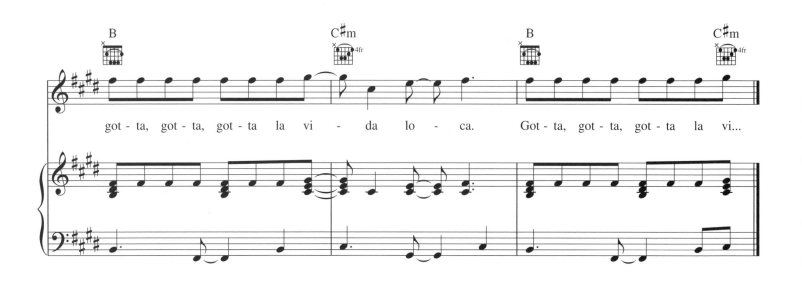

got-ta, got-ta, got-ta la vi - da lo - ca. Got-ta, got-ta, got-ta la vi...

THE RIVER OF DREAMS

Words and Music by
BILLY JOEL

Smooth Shuffle, with soul

Ooh,

ah;

ooh,

blind, _____ in the mid-dle of the night. _____
dreams, _____ in the mid-dle of the

LOSING MY RELIGION

Words and Music by BILL BERRY,
PETER BUCK, MIKE MILLS
and MICHAEL STIPE

MY HEART WILL GO ON
(Love Theme from 'Titanic')
from the Paramount and Twentieth Century Fox Motion Picture TITANIC

Music by JAMES HORNER
Lyric by WILL JENNINGS

Ev - 'ry night in my dreams I see you, I feel you, that is how I know you go on.

NOTHING COMPARES 2 U

Words and Music by
PRINCE

Noth - ing com-pares, nothing com-pares 2 U.

Nothing com-pares, __ nothing com-pares 2 U.

Repeat and Fade

ONE OF US

Words and Music by
ERIC BAZILIAN

SAVE THE BEST FOR LAST

Words and Music by WENDY WALDMAN,
PHIL GALDSTON and JON LIND

SMOOTH

Words by ROB THOMAS
Music by ROB THOMAS and ITAAL SHUR

TEARS IN HEAVEN

Words and Music by ERIC CLAPTON
and WILL JENNINGS

Be - yond   the   door ____   there's peace,   I'm   sure, ___

and I know ___ there'll be no more ___ tears in heav-

en.

D.S. al Coda

CODA

rall.

STREETS OF PHILADELPHIA

Words and Music by
BRUCE SPRINGSTEEN

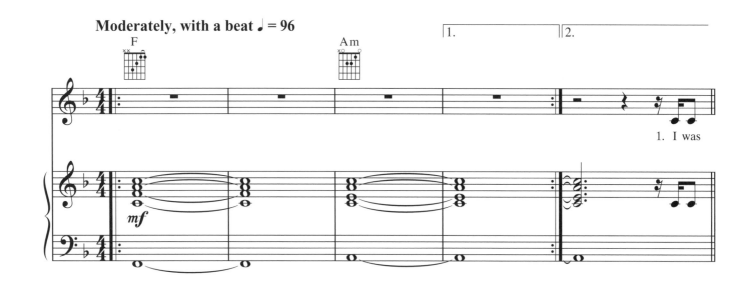

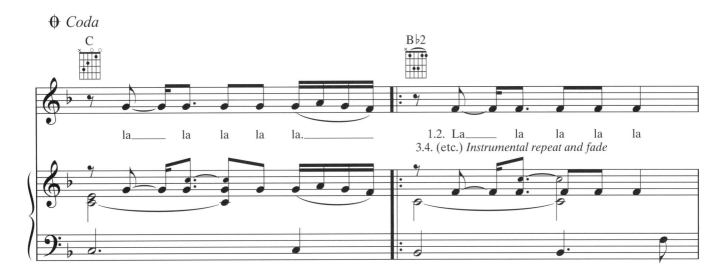

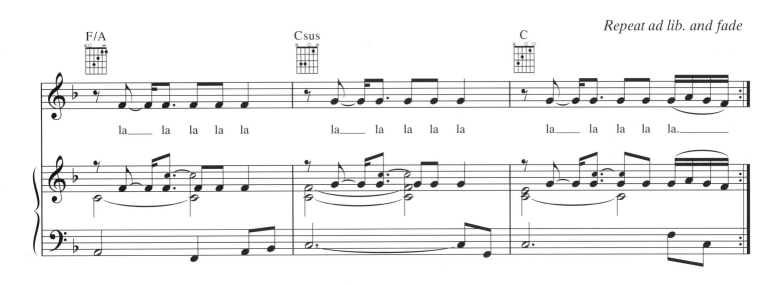

Verse 2:
I walked the avenue 'til my legs felt like stone.
I heard the voices of friends vanished and gone.
At night I could hear the blood in my veins
Just as black and whispering as the rain
On the streets of Philadelphia.
(To Chorus:)

Verse 3:
The night has fallen. I'm lyin' awake.
I can feel myself fading away.
So, receive me, brother, with your faithless kiss,
Or will we leave each other alone like this
On the streets of Philadelphia?
(To Chorus:)

SUNNY CAME HOME

Words and Music by SHAWN COLVIN
and JOHN LEVENTHAL

Moderately

Sun-ny came home to her fa-v'rite room. __ Sun-ny sat down in the

UNFORGETTABLE
(Duet Version)

Words and Music by
IRVING GORDON

UNPRETTY

Words and Music by DALLAS AUSTIN
and TIONNE WATKINS

Medium steady beat

I wish I could tie you up __ in my __ shoes, __ make you feel un - pret - ty, too.

Nev - er in - se - cure un - til __ I met __ you. __ Now I'm be - in' stu - pid.

Vocal line is written an octave higher than sung.

* *Vocal line is written as sung.*

VISION OF LOVE

Words and Music by MARIAH CAREY
and BEN MARGULIES

WALKING IN MEMPHIS

Words and Music by
MARC COHN

WHERE HAVE ALL THE COWBOYS GONE?

Words and Music by
PAULA COLE

Moderately fast Rock

Doo dit, doo doo dit, doo doo dit, doo doo dit, doo

doo dit, doo doo dit, doo doo dit, doo doo dit, doo doo dit, doo doo dit, doo

doo dit, doo doo dit, doo doo dit, doo doo dit, doo doo dit, doo doo.

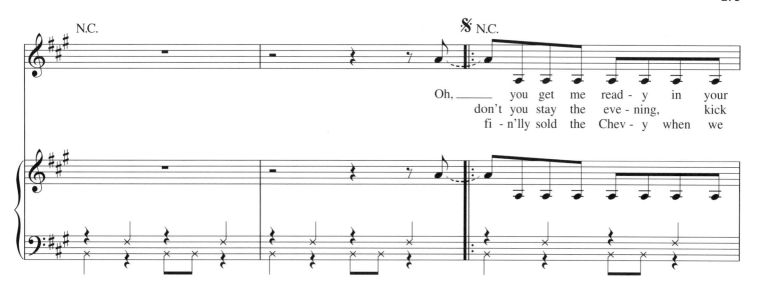

A WHOLE NEW WORLD
from Walt Disney's ALADDIN

Music by ALAN MENKEN
Lyrics by TIM RICE

YOU ARE NOT ALONE

Words and Music by
ROBERT KELLY

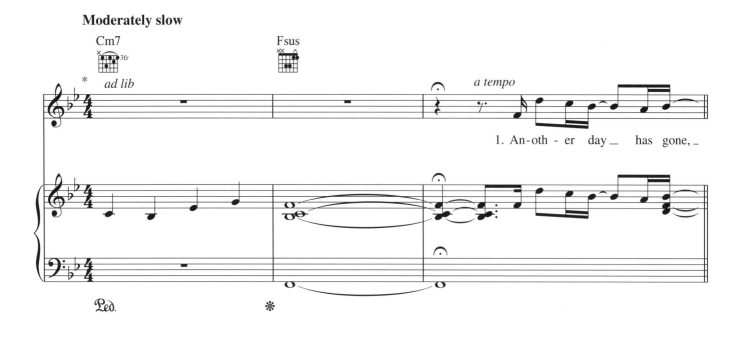

*Recorded a half step higher.

Additional lyrics

2. You are not alone
   I am here with you
   Though you're far away
   I am here to stay.
   You are not alone
   I am here with you
   Though we're far apart
   You're always in my heart.
   But you are not alone.

3. Just the other night
   I thought I heard you cry
   Asking me to go
   And hold you in my arms.
   I can hear your breaths
   Your burdens I will bear
   But first I need you here
   Then forever can begin.

4. You are not alone
   I am here with you
   Though you're far away
   I am here to stay.
   But you are not alone
   I am here with you
   Though we're far apart
   You're always in my heart.
   But you are not alone.

YOU'RE STILL THE ONE

Words and Music by SHANIA TWAIN
and R.J. LANGE

YOU'VE GOT A WAY

Words and Music by
SHANIA TWAIN and R.J. LANGE

Additional lyrics

3. You've got a way with words.
You get me smiling even when it hurts.
There's no way to measure what your love is worth.
I can't believe the way you get through to me.
To Chorus

YOU OUGHTA KNOW

Lyrics by ALANIS MORISSETTE
Music by ALANIS MORISSETTE
and GLEN BALLARD

Moderate Rock

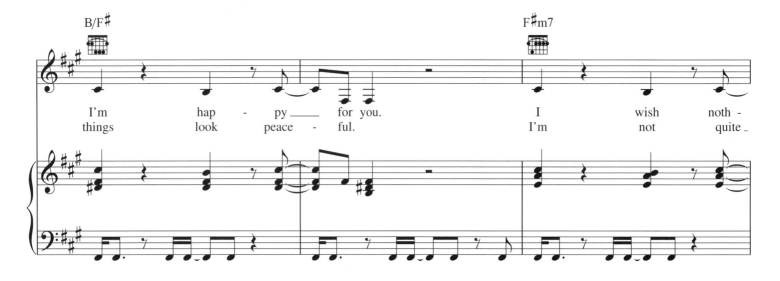